THIS BOOK

BELONGS TO

CREATE YOUR OWN JOURNAL ALL
ABOUT YOUR ADVENTURES IN SCHOOL.
WRITE, DRAW, STICK OR ASK ADULT
FOR HELP TO CREATE YOUR UNIQUE
MEMORY BOOK!

ABOUT ME

MY NAME

MY FAVORITE COLOUR

MY FAVORITE ANIMAL

MY FAVORITE GAME

MY PICTURE

MY TEACHER

MY TEACHER NAME

PICTURE

MY SCHOOL

MY SCHOOL NAME

_____

....

_____

MY FIRST DAY

I GO TO SCHOOL WITH

_____

....

_____

MY FIRST SCHOOL
LUNCHBOX

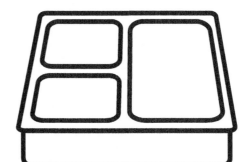

MY FIRST SCHOOL
BACKPACK

I FEEL

MY FIRST MEMORY

MY FIRST BOOK

MY FRIENDS

DATE

NAME

PICTURE

DATE

NAME

PICTURE

DATE

NAME

PICTURE

DATE

NAME

PICTURE

DATE

NAME

PICTURE

DATE

NAME

PICTURE

DATE

NAME

PICTURE

MY AMAZING MEMORIES

DATE

DAY

DATE

DAY

DATE

DAY

DATE

DAY

DATE

DAY

DATE

DAY

DATE

DAY

DATE

DAY

DATE	DAY

DATE

DAY

DATE

DAY

DATE

DAY

DATE

DAY

DATE

DAY

DATE

DAY

DATE

DAY

DATE

DAY

DATE

DAY

DATE

DAY

DATE

DAY

DATE

DAY

DATE

DAY

DATE

DAY

DATE

DAY

DATE

DAY

DATE

DAY

DATE

DAY

DATE

DAY

DATE

DAY

DATE

DAY

DATE

DAY

DATE

DAY

DATE

DAY

DATE

DAY

DATE

DAY

DATE

DAY

DATE

DAY

DATE

DAY

DATE

DAY

DATE	DAY

DATE

DAY

DATE

DAY

DATE

DAY

DATE

DAY

DATE

DAY

DATE

DAY

DATE

DAY

DATE

DAY

DATE

DAY

DATE

DAY

DATE

DAY

DATE

DAY

DATE

DAY

DATE

DAY

DATE

DAY

DATE

DAY

DATE

DAY

DATE

DAY

DATE

DAY

DATE

DAY

DATE

DAY

DATE

DAY

DATE

DAY

DATE

DAY

DATE

DAY

DATE

DAY

DATE

DAY

DATE

DAY

DATE

DAY

DATE

DAY

DATE	DAY

DATE

DAY

DATE

DAY

DATE

DAY

DATE

DAY

DATE

DAY

DATE

DAY

DATE

DAY

....

....

DATE

DAY

DATE

DAY

COLOURING

MY FIRST WRITING

CONNECT THE FARM ANIMALS

TRACE THE LETTERS

ALPHABET

Aa Bb Cc Dd Ee

Ff Gg Hh Ii Jj

Kk Ll Mm Nn

Oo Pp Qq Rr Ss

Tt Uu Vv Ww

Xx Yy Zz

TRACING NUMBERS

1   1   1   1   1

2   2   2   2   2

3   3   3   3   3

4   4   4   4   4

5   5   5   5   5

EMOTIONS!

SHAPES

SHAPES

SHADOW MATCHING

DAYS OF THE WEEK

Sunday

Monday

Tuesday

Wednesday

Thursday

Friday

Saturday

ALPHABET

Aa
is for apple

Bb
is for banana

Cc
is for cat

Dd
is for dog

Ee
is for egg

Ff
is for fish

Gg
is for gate

Hh
is for hat

Ii
is for igloo

Jj
is for jelly

Kk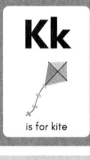
is for kite

Ll
is for lemon

Mm
is for monkey

Nn
is for net

Oo
is for orange

Pp
is for pear

Qq
is for queen

Rr
is for rabbit

Ss
is for strawberry

Tt
is for tiger

Uu
is for umbrella

Vv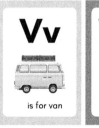
is for van

Ww
is for van

Xx
is for x-ray

Yy
is for yoyo

Zz
is for zebra

THANK YOU FOR YOUR PURCHASE!

IF YOU ENJOYED YOUR SHOPPING EXPERIENCE,
TELL US (AND OTHERS) ABOUT IT!

PLEASE, LEAVE YOUR REVIEW
IN COMMENT SECTION

Printed in Great Britain
by Amazon

83100192R00072